A Pearl
of Great Value

Women in Search of a Purposeful Life

A Pearl
of Great Value

Women in Search of a Purposeful Life

Linda M. Holub

WestBow
PRESS
A DIVISION OF THOMAS NELSON

To contact Linda Holub you can email at lholub@cableone.net or through her website at www.lifecoachingforsuccess.net

WestBow Press books may be ordered through booksellers or by contacting:

WestBow Press
A Division of Thomas Nelson
1663 Liberty Drive
Bloomington, IN 47403
www.westbowpress.com
1-(866) 928-1240

ISBN: 978-1-4497-1534-2 (sc)
ISBN: 978-1-4497-1536-6 (dj)
ISBN: 978-1-4497-1535-9 (e)

Library of Congress Control Number: 2011926314

Printed in the United States of America

WestBow Press rev. date: 5/19/2011

Table of Contents

Preface

God has impressed upon my heart that there is a need to encourage women to see themselves through God's eyes. A quote from St. Augustine emphasizes the high value God places on his relationship with you, "God loves each of us as if there were only one of us." Coming from a family of five children, God's personal care for me is invaluable to my feeling of significance. I have been inspired by the Holy Spirit to help women acquire their value from God's view of them. When I taught the principles in this book to a community college class, I was amazed by their personal growth through simply showing the women I believed in them and their abilities to fulfill their God-given life purpose.

The true strength to live a God-given purposeful life lies in our belief in what God says in His word about God's redeemed people. Who are the redeemed? In Ephesians 1:7-8, the Apostle Paul tells us, "In him we have redemption through his blood, the forgiveness of sins, in accordance with the riches of God's grace that he lavished on us with all wisdom and understanding." Redemption means you have been bought with the blood of Jesus Christ from the penalty for sin which is death and reconciled you to God. On our own power, we fail, lose steam and revert to our own human understanding of our capacity to accomplish the work God has ordained for us. On our own we fall short of what God envisions for our lives.

We all continuously need an infusion of encouragement to grab hold of a God-sized belief that we were made to have a significant impact in our world for God's glory. Is that true of you?

God has allowed me the privilege of seeing the growth in these women. I count it pure joy and a blessing, and I look forward to hearing how God will speak to your heart as you begin to peel back the layers of your own life.

Acknowledgments

First, I give God the glory, *Soli Deo Gloria,* for what He has enabled me to write. Without God feeding me the words, this manuscript would not have been completed. I recognize my husband for his support of my journey to live my God-given life purpose. Without his support, I would be in a far different place today. I dedicate this book to my four children, Chris, Trisha, Bria and Jaime and my son-in-law, Kevin. I pray they will discover and live their God-given life purpose that satisfies the soul like no other.

I thank my friends who have given me unbelievable encouragement to pursue sharing these principles and assured me it would add value to others. Cheri Maben-Crouch, PhD., a fellow life purpose coach, has been an amazing encourager, without whom I would not have gone forward with this project. I give due recognition to Brent Hoffman who has been truly helpful because of his amazing editing skills.

In addition, I want to express my appreciation to Ta'Mara Hanscom for opening up options for publishing. She has written and published her own series of Christian novels. Sharing her experience with me shortened my learning curve.

Finally, I thank my mother, who has proven in her life that life experiences are more valuable than formal education. She also showed me that age need not be a factor when you launch a new career or accept a new challenge, regardless of the prevailing societal wisdom. We could also learn this from whom Jesus chose as His disciples, an uneducated group of men He equipped through the Holy Spirit to change the world forever.

Prologue

*I*n *autumn 2007, Sarah was at her wits end. Her husband was in the prime of his business life, busy with exciting opportunities coming his way every day, it seemed. Sarah's children had finished college and were involved in their own lives. To say she was suffering from empty-nest syndrome would be to underestimate the pit of loneliness in which she found herself.*

Sarah thought she was too old to return to school, even though she was always a good student. She believed she had to weigh the financial investment with the financial return she would receive by starting a new career. "Can I justify going back to school?" she thought.

Her husband questioned the viability of it as well. His questioning created even more doubt in Sarah's mind as to whether she was worth the investment. She remembered enjoying writing in college, but she wondered, "Who really cares what I think anyway? What do I have to offer other people?"

Sarah was stuck in an unfulfilling life, not trusting that she had anything of value to offer. She often questioned her value in the lives of her family and in society as a whole. Sarah confided to a church friend that she was feeling lost and insignificant. Her friend listened patiently, hearing Sarah's heartfelt desire to somehow contribute to society.

Knowing Sarah was floundering on her own, her friend recommended a Christian life coach. Sarah decided to interview this coach and learn about life coaching. She liked the fact that coaching was a partnership with her to take her from Point A, where she was that day, to Point B, where she wanted her life to go, and she hired the life coach.

Within the first month, the coach had Sarah defining her values and evaluating whether she was living in harmony with those values. Sarah realized how important her faith was to her wellbeing, but also recognized she was starving her faith by the way she spent her time. Upon reevaluation, she restructured her schedule to spend more time with God, the author of her life and life purpose. Through changes to her agenda, Sarah could explore her strengths and passions to see where God would direct the next season of her life.

Recalling how much she had enjoyed writing in college led to a new found confidence to write extemporaneously. Soon thereafter, Sarah applied for a job as a writer with a monthly magazine her city newspaper published. She was now putting her faith to work in writing spiritual lessons through every day events with which the average person could relate. Having found a fulfilling niche, she felt renewed vigor to live her life to the fullest. It was amazing how much better she felt once she identified her God-given purpose for this season of her life.

Can you relate to Sarah's season of discontent? Do you question your value to society and to God? Perhaps you wonder if there is more to life than what you are experiencing. God wants you to experience the abundant life He has planned for you, but it requires connecting intimately to the life giver, Jesus.

This book will help you find your life purpose and live life to the fullest. God did not create you for mediocrity, but, rather, for power and influence in the world. Continue reading to see how you can discover your God-given life purpose. God knows your name and your struggles. God knows the pearl of great value He has placed in you. Trust God to guide you in that revelation.

"Again, the kingdom of heaven is like a merchant looking for fine pearls. When he found one of great value, he went away and sold everything he had and bought it."

Matthew 13:46

Beginning the Journey

Have you ever wondered how the magnificent pearl is created? Have you marveled at its beauty? The life journey of the pearl is not an easy path. It begins when an irritant finds its way into the oyster. Just as you might well expect, an irritant is not a pleasant experience for the oyster. The word "irritant" creates an image of pain and discomfort for the oyster.

I liken this irritant to the thorn in the Apostle Paul's side that we read about in II Corinthians 12: 7-9. We know that this thorn was painful because the Apostle Paul asked God three times to remove it. However, God told him His grace was sufficient for him and thus, God did not remove the thorn. God must have had a greater purpose for Paul with the continued presence of the thorn than with it removed. In the same way, if the irritant is not expelled, there is a greater purpose when left to full maturation, a beautiful pearl emerges.

The pearl, created through this painful process, is very different from a mass-produced or man-made pearl. It has what the gem industry would call "imperfections", whereas the man-made pearls are perfectly symmetrical and their surface is very smooth. I consider these "imperfections" to be the uniqueness of each individually crafted pearl. In the same way, you are unique; you have your own essence – that is, the pearl within you.

You are a pearl of great value as you desire to follow your God-given path that God created for you. Does it make sense, then, that if you are to be a pearl of great value, you may experience stress and uncomfortable times as you are chiseled and molded into a person of integrity and humility whom God can use for His purposes?

God desires to make us complete but that doesn't happen through a stress-free life. A stress-free life isn't possible in this sin-ravaged world which steals our joy and compassion and hardens our hearts.

In my life journey, I continue to be deeply saddened as I meet women who feel powerless to change their lives. Often, they are overwhelmed with unfulfilling, meaningless tasks. They see little value in what they can offer. Somewhere in their experiences with their significant others, they quit trusting their instincts and valuing their uniqueness. As a result, they conclude that they don't deserve the opportunity to dream their own dreams or blaze their own trails. They become stuck in a life of mediocrity and listlessness.

The Psalmist (16:11) tells us what God intends to do for us, "You will make known to me the path of life; you will fill me with joy in your presence, with eternal pleasures at your right hand." You may say, "I want that." You can have that if you seek the LORD with all your heart.

The foundation of being stuck is feeling that you have no control over your life. I want you to know that there is more life to be lived. You have the power to change the direction of your life if you lean on God's power and then take back the reins from whomever you have given the control.

Each new season of life opens up new opportunities for living a life of significance and purpose. I saw this early in my life, and it helped me be content during each season knowing it wouldn't last forever. I did not take the path most traveled as a young adult because it did not fit within my value system. What that meant for me was finding the courage to swim against the current and finding the resolve to stand firm in my convictions. It did take courage and determination to refuse to follow what had become a postmodern militant women's rights career track. I chose to be a stay-at-home mom for 15 years as my four children grew up. Society does not affirm going against the current. However, as God has allowed, I have made that transition many times in a struggle to live in harmony with my values.

I began a career in social work after college. When I went through my first pregnancy, I decided I would not be living within my value system if I worked fulltime outside the home. I decided to stay home to care for my children. I did that for 15 years. When you make a major decision like this, you must be prepared to live on much less income, requiring many sacrifices. I was willing to commit to that lifestyle and trust God would provide for our needs, and He did.

When you follow your value system, it doesn't mean you will avoid pitfalls. Nor does it mean those around you necessarily appreciate the sacrifices you are making. Being committed to staying home did give me the resolve I needed to stand firm during the most difficult times. Living in harmony with your values provides a tremendous peace of mind.

When I decided to return to work, I reinvented myself by entering into real estate sales. I worked around my children's schedule as much as was possible and worked in that industry successfully for 13 years. God had been coaxing me to retire from real estate. Whenever I heard a sermon asking what is taking you away from time with God, my answer was "work".

I rejected the notion of quitting because I remembered the sacrifices we had to make when I stayed home with my children. I had come to enjoy the pleasures my extra money gave us. Eventually, however, I had the courage to retire, knowing extra money would be scarce. When I retired from real estate sales, my youngest of four children was in college. I was again making a financial decision to live on less income, but I was also choosing to honor my values. I did not want my legacy to be that I accumulated wealth and possessions. With the schedule I kept in real estate and caring for four children, I had no time or energy to do anything else of significance. This is not to say you couldn't, but it was clear I lacked the energy it required. I wanted to make a significant difference in my world, but I had no idea what form that would take.

Since then, I have reinvented myself several times. I say this to encourage you. If I can do it, you can reinvent yourself and live a more purposeful life. In order to redirect your life successfully, you need to know your values, strengths and passions. They form your firm foundation which then, creates a confidence to make decisions. They become your internal compass. Without a compass you live with chaos and insecurity as you are tossed by the winds of societal whims. Not only do you have chaos in your mind, but also, in our fast-paced society, chaos reigns in every sphere of your life.

God set His values in you at your creation. God intended for you to allow Him to be your internal Global Positioning System (GPS). As our GPS, God can redirect us when we go off course. We get a course correction if we are listening. For example, sometimes God closes doors to get my attention. I often need to be hit with a well-placed two by four to get the picture because of my strong-willed nature. Because of this, I frequently pray God will change my husband's mind if this is the way I am to go; in that way, his attitude about the subject will be a confirmation for me that God is directing me toward this path.

Isn't it wonderful that God personalizes His guidance to what works best for each of us? We have a very personal God. God longs to have a relationship with us. Out of God's amazing love for us, He never gets weary wooing us to Himself. In Isaiah 40:11, we see how tenderly God feels toward us as He is compared to a shepherd caring for his sheep. Listen to these words, "He tends his flock like a shepherd: he gathers the lambs in his arms and carries them close to his heart; he gently leads those that have young." Is this a God you can trust with your life, your hurts, and your desires? Will you ask God for His wisdom to direct your life purpose?

What do you believe about God's interest in you, in particular? Can you believe the Sovereign God, Creator of the universe, pauses to care about your life? The Psalmist (147: 4) tells us, "He determines the number of the stars and calls them each by name." Some say the number of stars is 10 to the 22nd[1]. If God named each star, I pray you know God cares much more for you. God knows your name. You are precious in His sight.

If your self-esteem is not cloaked in God's love, you will be swayed by the taunting words of the evil one who spews lies, causing you to distrust God's view of your value. Basing your self-worth on anything but God's love will result in crumbling under the assault of the evil one. In John 10:10, we see the true intent of the evil one, "The thief comes only to steal and kill and destroy; I have come that they may have life, and have it to the full."

If you could believe in God's intimate, personal knowledge of you and God's commitment to give you a hope and a future (Jeremiah

29:11), you would gain tremendous power to weather the ups and downs of life.

God created you with desires and passions for a purpose. Listen to what David says in Psalms 37:4, "Delight yourself in the LORD and he will give you the desires of your heart." God wants you to be all God created you to be. Can you grasp the concept that you are valuable, unique and special to God? Can you grasp that God has ordained a purpose chosen just for you?

I believe you want to live a life of significance or you wouldn't be reading this book. I believe God has created you with the intellect, the abilities and the passion to fulfill your God-given purpose. Those gifts are the tools "through which God's Spirit channels divine love, mercy, and power into the lives of other people resulting in growth for the Body of Christ and glory for God" (*My 50-Day Journey to Empowered Living* by John Carnett, Sam Farina, Tim Hoog and Paul Kolbeck, p 54).

When you use your gifts, you become the vessel through which God's blessings affect those around you. By the time you finish reading this book, I pray you will believe in yourself as an instrument of God. God created you as a powerful force for good to influence the world and to give God glory.

In order for you to move forward toward your life purpose, you will need to engage in the self-discovery process by actually completing the exercises provided for you. Otherwise, it becomes a theoretical self-help book which never transforms lives. This self-discovery process will unfold, a little at a time, your authentic self. I recommend you take the journey with a group of friends or a small group of women. The group will hold each of you accountable to complete the exercises but also to give you affirmation and confirmation on what you are discovering about yourself. There are no shortcuts in this discovery process. It will take courage to take advantage of the discoveries you will uncover by making new decisions, but the mere fact that you have picked up this book tells me you are eager to pursue your best life.

It may surprise you to know that your beliefs govern your behavior. This is an important concept to grasp as you evaluate your life and look to make changes. To illustrate this point, I ask you to think back to a time you may have been involved in a team building exercise. The goal of these exercises is to get people to trust one another.

A popular activity is asking one person to trust the rest of the group to catch him or her when he or she falls backward toward the ground. If you did not believe your teammates were strong enough or committed enough to hold you, would you even consider trying this exercise? I don't think so. Because you believe they are strong enough and like you enough to catch you, you are willing to play the game.

To illustrate this further, I remember several years ago a friend of mine encouraged me to go rollerblading with her. I was in my 50's. My friend was just a couple of years older than me. I am usually game for an adventure. I decided to try rollerblading because I believed I was as physically fit as she so I concluded I could do it too. Now if a 30 year old friend had suggested I try it, my belief system may not have been strong enough to push me to try it because there is a great deal difference in our physical abilities. It was my belief system that allowed me to try something new. Are you getting the idea how important your belief system is in governing your behavior?

David Stoop[2] (2009) in his book, *You Are What You Think,* recounted an experiment that "Dr. Aaron Beck, one of the early theorists who advocated the treatment of depression by changing a person's Self-Talk, developed…. In the group working only on their self-talk, over seventy-five percent showed a complete recovery." If clinically depressed patients can be healed by positive self-talk, imagine the impact on your life if you began a habit of positive self-talk. Your attitudes are based on your belief system. To further illustrate this point, if I think I have been treated unfairly, my attitude is likely to be negative. I may then take a negative action based on my attitude, which is based on the belief that I was treated unfairly.

Your belief system affects all your relationships. Consider this. If you are convinced someone is a true friend who likes and respects you, you probably will have a different reaction to them if he or she says something that offends you. You may give that person a pass, thinking they misspoke.

However, what happens if someone whom you do not believe likes you said the same thing? You probably will react negatively and will be deeply offended. What is different about these two circumstances? The only difference was your belief about each person. Does this make sense? If so, how would knowing your beliefs affect your behavior, influence what you think and say to yourself in the form of self-talk?

We will discuss strategies to help you counteract negative self-talk in a later chapter. Henry Ford said, "If you believe you can or you believe you can't, you are right." That statement exemplifies how what you believe translates into behavior as a self-fulfilling prophesy. This illustrates the importance of knowing what you believe and focusing on thinking positive thoughts.

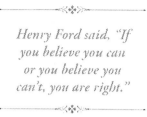

Henry Ford said, "If you believe you can or you believe you can't, you are right."

Those positive thoughts come from what we feed our minds. The Word of God is the most effective tool against negative self-talk. It is mightier than any two-edged sword in fighting the evil one who is the author of the lies. God's Word, which is truth, cuts through Satan's lies.

We all need encouragement. For example, how would your life be different if you had heard, "I believe in you" as you were growing up? Do you think your goals for your life might have been on a higher level? Words like, "I know you can do it" or "you have what it takes to be successful in whatever you want to do with your life". Words of encouragement fuel our desire to be the best we can be. I do believe in you and your ability to live a purposeful life because I know God has equipped you perfectly for your life purpose.

You may not see any way God can use your checkered past. However, God never wastes your tears or failures. God loves a repentant heart and is eager to forgive and heal those who come to Him in repentance. In 1 John 1:9 we read, "If we confess our sins, he is faithful and just and will forgive us our sins and purify us from all unrighteousness." God uses your failures to help someone facing similar circumstances.

Have you ever been helped by knowing someone has gone through the same trauma you have experienced? God uses you by allowing you to help someone going through similar situations. If someone has had a comparable experience to yours, he or she will be a better support system. In the process, you develop a new friendship. C.S. Lewis said,

"Friendship is born at the moment when one person says to another: "What? You, too? I thought I was the only one.""

Jim Cymbala said, "Faith never denies reality but leaves room for God to grant a new reality." Do you allow God an opportunity to create a new reality for you? What new reality awaits you? How might it look? Take a risk and ask God to show you what you were created to do.

Perhaps you feel unworthy or insignificant. Your self-esteem has taken a toll because life has been hard and you may feel broken by life experiences. You do not believe you are special. I want to encourage you to see yourself through God's eyes. David writes in Psalm 139:13-14, "For you created my inmost being; you knit me together in my mother's womb. I praise you because I am fearfully and wonderfully made; your works are wonderful. I know that full well." God was intimately involved in your creation to the point of getting His hands in the dirt. God formed humanity from the dust of the ground. That is love, and that is personal!

One way to understand this concept is to think of God as the potter and we are the clay. I have had the privilege to experience using a potter's wheel. A friend took the time to teach me this process. She was very skilled at it but I learned I was not. I enjoyed the challenge, however. It is difficult to create something distinguishable from the clay. It involves beginning with a big block of clay and kneading vigorously to remove the air holes. Next, you must center the clay on a continuously moving wheel. That requires placing heavy pressure on the clay and forces you to use your whole body to do the task.

The centering process is complicated by the centrifugal force that can cause it to dislodge from the wheel and fly off uncontrollably, much like Satan tries to dislodge you from focusing on God's will for your life. If Satan is successful, your life is out of control like the flying clay. If the clay is not centered, it cannot be molded.

In the same way, God cannot shape and mold you unless you are centered on and surrendered to God. God does not force anyone to follow Him. God gave us free will to choose to or not to love and follow Him. Going back to the clay analogy, once the clay is centered, through a process of placing various degrees of pressure on it, it begins to take shape. Finally, you have created something useful and identifiable.

I liken the application of pressure to the struggles we face in life. God handpicks the struggles that we will face depending on our personalities and what God knows we can handle. God promises that we will not face anything too difficult for us to handle with His help. However, God may take you all the way to the edge of what you can handle. When we are on that edge, we are more likely to look to God for help. We will all have struggles, and our response to those struggles shape our lives.

Allow me to return to the potter analogy. By the end of the process, I was highly invested in my clay project and was very proud and protective of the small bowl I created. God feels the same kind of parental protective feeling toward you. Your heavenly Father's love for you is far beyond your ability to understand. It comes in the form of care, protection, provision, healing, companionship, and filling your soul with feelings of wholeness.

To glimpse God's love, consider your love for your children or other significant people in your life. Your love is only a shadow of God's love. My love for my children penetrates to my core. I would move mountains if I thought it would benefit my children. Can you grasp that our love is only a shadow of the real thing?

God's love is all encompassing. How does that help you to know that? For me, to know God's love is everything. My worth is wrapped up in that truth. God doesn't make junk. That was the cornerstone of my self-worth from the day I accepted Christ as my Savior. That means I am worthy of God's love. It was not because of anything I did. Christ did it all for me, dying on that cross for my sins of yesterday, today and tomorrow.

If we ever doubt that our creation is anything but awesome, we need only look at our amazing physical bodies to conclude that we are indeed a special creation. When I consider the delicate balance and the interdependence of the inner workings of my body, I am totally in awe of God's created beings.

Having this knowledge of how special we are helps me to keep fighting the good fight when the world seems against me. I remember God's personal involvement in my creation. Knowing how personal my God is keeps me from falling into the miry pit of insignificance and self-pity. Could that knowledge help you to believe in your value?

In Matthew 7:9-11, you learn how much God cares for you, "Which of you, if his son asks for bread, will give him a stone? Or if he asks for a fish, will give him a snake? If you, then, though you are evil, know how to give good gifts to your children, how much more will your Father in heaven give good gifts to those who ask him!"

Grab hold of God's love and your uniqueness and run with it. Believe it! My heart goes out to those who feel of so little value. The truth is: you are of great value-- a precious pearl in God's eyes.

God has given me a passion for empowering women with the knowledge that they are Christ's creation, a work of art, to do great things God has prepared them to do. God has not planned an insignificant life for you but, rather, one of great power and influence for God's glory. I do not want to give the impression that the great life God has planned is just to feed our egos because that is not at all why we are given such great promises. It is always to further God's glory.

The truth is: you are of great value-- a precious pearl in God's eyes.

Looking for God's leading will give you unbelievable life experiences that will enrich your life. You have an opportunity to decide what legacy you will leave for your family and friends. What will you use your time on earth to do? Live in victory, fulfill your God–given purpose or hide in mediocrity?

The goal of this book is to help women develop a new identity based on their faith in Jesus Christ, using their passions and their dreams to fulfill their life purpose. I pray you will discover the God-given pearl of great value within you. The pearl is the essence of you which God intends for you to share with the world.

Jesus told the father of the demon-possessed boy, ... "Everything is possible for him who believes." *(Mark 9:23)* Do you feel powerless today? You can choose to live by faith and in God's power today, but will you?

Believing something is possible is the beginning of a dream. Then it grows to be a vision that produces action to accomplish your dream. No one makes concerted effort toward something they believe is unlikely to happen.

Where should you begin? If you have not yet accepted God's gift of salvation, I suggest you begin there. With God, all things are possible, without God, all is meaningless. When you submit to your Creator,

God rewards you and responds to your heart's desire. Without Christ, we are powerless to be who we were created to be. All humanity was made to desire to belong. You can belong to Christ's family today if you choose to accept His gift of salvation. Pray with me.

Dear Jesus,

I know I am a sinner with no hope on my own of measuring up to your standards. I am guilty of evil thoughts and behaviors toward others. I want to turn from my wicked ways. I believe you sent your perfect Son, Jesus Christ, to earth and to the cross to pay the cost for my sins. I believe Jesus arose, ascended into heaven and defeated death and its sting. Please come into my life and guide and direct my path as the Lord of my life. In your precious name, I pray, Amen.

We are taking a journey together. Your bags are packed. Each chapter will unpack your essence, your authentic self. Through the process of discovery, you will experience change in your perspective on life. You will peel away one layer at a time as you discover your values, strengths, passions and purpose. Until you have done the work in each chapter, you cannot unveil the "authentic" you.

Join me on this journey and commit to risk stepping out of your comfort zone each and every day by making new decisions. In the next chapter we will look objectively at your life as it is today and evaluate the level of your satisfaction with your life. Enjoy the process the Lord is setting before you. Hear these words from Isaiah 40:31, "But those who hope in the LORD will renew their strength. They will soar on wings like eagles; they will run and not grow weary, they will walk and not be faint."

*"Let us examine our ways and test them,
and let us return to the LORD."*

Lamentations 3:40

*"Before I formed you in the womb I knew you, before
you were born I set you apart..." Jeremiah 1:5a*

My Life Today

You may have less than fond memories of your childhood. Life may not have been kind to you thus far. I understand that to be true for many reading this book. I have compassion for where you have been. I have had some very rugged spots in my life as well. As difficult as those rough places were, I realize that sometimes only through hardship do we mature and experience personal and spiritual growth. In James 1:2-4, we are told, "Consider it pure joy, my brothers, whenever you face trials of many kinds, because you know that the testing of your faith develops perseverance. Perseverance must finish its work so that you may be mature and complete, not lacking anything."

Through suffering, I begin to understand to a very small degree the sufferings of Christ. If my loved ones hurt me, do I remember how many evil things I have done that hurt God? If God suffers, is it reasonable to think I will suffer as I try to follow God's ways? I pray that you will use your life journey, rough or smooth, to catapult you forward to realize the awesome life God has ordained for you.

Do you remember having fun in your childhood with a kaleidoscope? I like the word picture of a kaleidoscope to describe your life journey. The bright and cheerful colors represent the joyous times. The more subdued colors are times of sadness and loss, but as you turn the canister, they blend together to become the beautiful picture of who you are today. Picture your life journey as a tapestry, where each experience is a thread weaving a tapestry of your life. When it is finished, it is a beautiful work of art, God's masterpiece.

Picture your life journey as a tapestry, where each experience is a thread weaving a tapestry of your life.

As the first step in this journey, you will have the opportunity to look at who you are now and to what you devote your time and energy. Then, you will evaluate those things to see if they reflect your priorities. You may find you are not spending your time on your priorities. You will then have the opportunity to plan and plant your perennial garden or your future life. You will be able to weed out worry and negative thinking and plant kindness, compassion, self-confidence and all things positive.

In this first exercise, you will begin to unpack the authentic you. The process will enable you to visualize what consumes your time each week. It will provide an opportunity to evaluate whether this reflects your priorities. It is a starting point for measuring your progress as well. The following exercise is one way to look objectively at your life. Each exercise peels away a layer at a time, allowing for new discoveries and then, new decision about your life.

The goal of this first exercise is to draw a tree that shows the roles you play and the number of people for whom you are responsible. It will offer you an overall picture of what occupies your time.

Exercise:

1. List all the roles you play that take at least one hour a week of your time. You may be a mother, a daughter, a sister, an aunt, a volunteer, an employee, a committee chair, an employer, a Bible study leader, or someone else.

   _____

   _____

   _____

   _____

   _____

2. Begin by drawing a tree trunk on the next page, which represents you. Each branch will represent a role you play. Be sure the size of the branch represents the amount of time you spend in each role. For instance, if you are a mother of small children, the branch representing motherhood will be almost as large as the tree trunk. But if you are a grandmother who lives a fair distance from your grandchildren, the branch as grandparent will be smaller than it would be for a young mother. The leaves will represent the people you are responsible for in that role. Ladies, this is not an art project so please give yourself some grace; it won't matter what your tree looks like.

TREE

Now answer the following questions:

1. What did you learn or re-learn from this exercise?

    _____

    _____

    _____

    _____

2. What surprised you?

    _____

    _____

    _____

    _____

3. In what ways does this tree represent your priorities?

    _____

    _____

    _____

    _____

    _____

    _____

    _____

    _____

4. In what ways is it in harmony with what you believe your values to
    be? In what ways is it not in harmony with your values?

    _____

    _____

    _____

    _____

5. What energy drainers did you identify? What do you need to do to find time for the things you desire to do such as hobbies or volunteer work?

   _____

   _____

   _____

   _____

6. How would you re-create your TREE to represent your priorities and interest areas? What action steps can you take to get there? What action steps can you take to eliminate, delegate or re-structure to give you the time you need to do the things you long to do?

   _____

   _____

   _____

   _____

The tree trunk is the channel of strength for the tree. It is the tree's foundation. What happens to the people to whom you are responsible when your strength is zapped from energy draining activities? You are your family's foundation because God created women with a heart for family. The tree gets its strength from the life giver: the roots. It needs nourishment and rest to be strong and to fulfill its purpose. The branches may dry up from internal rottenness or lack of nutrition.

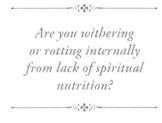

Are you withering or rotting internally from lack of spiritual nutrition?

What is feeding you spiritually? Are you withering or rotting internally from lack of spiritual nutrition? The only way to avoid withering internally is to be connected to God, our source of life and nourishment.

Jesus tells us in John 15:5, "I am the vine; you are the branches. If a man remains in me and I in him, he will bear much fruit; apart from me you can do nothing." God's nourishment is sufficient for us to bear fruit, but nothing else allows you to bear fruit that is enduring.

As you have looked at what occupies your time and energy, I pray you can see the choices you can make, decisions that will put you in harmony with your priorities. You are not stuck in this place unless you wish to be. You hold the reins to intentional living. What will you do with what you have learned? Decide today to take a risk and move in the direction of your priorities.

Dear Heavenly Father, you created me in your image. Please enlighten the eyes of my heart to get in touch with those values you have placed in me and help me live in harmony with them. I want to please you in the way I live. I want to experience the joy and blessings of living a God-focused life. Please guide and direct my path. Thank you for the love you lavish on me. In your almighty name I pray. Amen.

"For by the grace given me I say to every one of you: Do not think of yourself more highly than you ought, but rather think of yourself with sober judgment, in accordance with the measure of faith God has given you." Romans 12:3

Examining Your Level of
Satisfaction in Your Life

Do you feel frustrated, insignificant and long for a more fulfilling life, yet you don't have a clue what to do to make that happen? You are not alone. One method of discovering what that means for you is to do an objective self-evaluation. This is a foreign concept to most people. Perhaps, it is a fear of what they will find or the fear of making a change that prevents this process from happening.

Socrates, the Greek philosopher, said, "The unexamined life is not worth living." If we never examine our lives, we will not learn from our mistakes or learn to handle things better in the future. Self-examination is healthy and motivates us to change something we may have tolerated too long and need to change.

When you take the time to objectively look at your life, you may find you are functioning well in some areas, while in others you are woefully falling short of your expectations. That is not unusual. However, to live the life God ordained for you begins with contentment in each area of your life.

> *Socrates, the Greek philosopher, said, "The unexamined life is not worth living."*

Contentment does not mean life is perfect. It means you are comfortable that God has you at this place in your life for a reason. The perfect peace about which Jesus speaks does not depend on circumstances but in knowing in whom and in what you believe and then living in harmony with those beliefs. Circumstances change; but our attitude about the circumstances determines our level of peace. That we choose our attitudes is a harsh reality to face.

I have struggled in my life with attitudes. For a time, I was angry and did not want to take responsibility for choosing a negative view of my circumstances. Still, God put people in my life to warn me of the dangers of this path. Odd as it sounds, sometimes, we enjoy our bad attitudes and get so much pleasure out of them that we don't want to let go. I did not realize how my attitude affected those closest to me. A negative attitude is a poison that permeates relationships. I had some things to learn about that anger before I could move on.

Do you believe God has placed you where you are and wants you to learn something from your circumstances? God never misses an opportunity for a teachable moment. Could that be the case for where you are now? Or have you chosen not to move forward because of fear or insecurity about the unknown?

Todd Duncan (1999) in his book, *The Power to Be Your Best*, said, "The path is life. The vehicle is you. The fuel is your belief system, which is supported by the principles upon which you build your life." Does this make sense to you? Do you know someone whose belief in the possibility of meeting a goal is so strong that nothing will persuade him or her to change course? When I am convinced I need to act, I will move heaven and earth to accomplish it without regard to those who say it's impossible. That is passion fueled by belief.

Our belief system is our fuel. It energizes us. My belief system kept me moving forward during the most difficult times in my life. I could have given up, but I believed, even at my lowest point, that if I just hung in there another day it would be better tomorrow. Without that belief, I don't think I could have gotten up each and every day with the desire to do my best that day.

How do you keep moving forward? You need to keep your tank full of fuel. The way to keep a full tank of fuel is to feed on the Word of God which encourages you and feeds your soul. It re-energizes your belief system and guides you in living in harmony with it. Few people take the time to examine their lives and then make the decision to live and act intentionally in a way that is in agreement with their values.

Jesus offers us the ability to thrive not just make it through the next day, the next month or the next year. Webster defines thrive as to prosper, to progress toward or realize a goal. I think we all want to not only thrive but to flourish. Take a deeper look at your life today in its totality. Here is the Wheel of Life[3] exercise to help you.

1. Draw a large circle. Divide it into eight pie pieces by making four diagonal lines through the circle which creates eight lines within the circle. On each diagonal line, mark 10 evenly spaced lines beginning with one at the center of the circle and ending with 10 on the outside edge of the circle.

2. Label each section with one of the following categories: family relationships, finances, career, spirituality, personal development, social relationships, health, physical environment or leisure time (which ever fits your life more accurately).

3. Look at each of the eight areas of your life as it is today and place a dot on the number between one and 10 which best describes your level of satisfaction in each area. Again, one is at the center of the circle representing the least satisfied and 10 is most satisfied.

Wheel of Life

4. After giving each area a score that measures your level of satisfaction, connect the dots. Are you rolling along smoothly or are you moving along in a disjointed, uneven vehicle?

    _____

    _____

    _____

5. What did you learn or re-learn from this? What things are you tolerating that need to change?

    _____

    _____

    _____

    _____

    _____

    _____

Duncan also said, "To change your life you must engage in new choices and make different decisions." Einstein said, "Insanity is doing the same thing over and over again and expecting different results."

> *"To change your life you must engage in new choices and make different decisions."*

To stop the merry-go-round of your life from going in the same direction, do the following: for each area that is not a 10, write three action steps that you can take to improve your level of satisfaction. Remember the action steps should be incremental, measurable steps to prevent getting frustrated and giving up. This example may help you. When I had a lapse in an exercise program, to get back on track, I will go on the treadmill and raise the elevation level one or two levels and the same with the speed until I get back to where I was before the lapse. It prevented me from giving up or overdoing it and being in pain and agony. At the same time, stretch yourself by taking a risk; do something you have never done before.

Before you begin, take time to visualize what a 10 would look like in this area of your life; then you will be ready to create action steps to lead you to a 10 in that area.

If you are looking to lose weight to improve your health, you may want to begin by creating a food journal to allow you to first see what you are eating daily. Secondly, you could look at that list of foods and decide what you will eliminate for one week. Thirdly, the next week choose another food you can take out of your diet. Or, if you want to be more responsible financially, you may decide to keep track of all that you spend each week by writing it down. You can, then, decide what on that list you can do without for a week. The third step may be taking one more purchase out of your budget, maybe that latte you buy daily. Does that give you an idea of what I am looking for here?

Area: _____

_____

_____

_____

_____

Area: _____

_____

_____

_____

_____

Area: _____

_____

_____

_____

_____

Area: _____

_____

_____

_____

_____

_____

Area: _____

_____

_____

_____

_____

_____

Area: _____

_____

_____

_____

_____

Area: _____

_____

_____

_____

_____

Area: _____

_____

_____

_____

_____

Will you commit to taking these steps you have outlined as ways to improve your satisfaction in each area of your life? Change only happens when you make new decisions. It does take courage to take these incremental steps but it will be well worth the effort. Each time you take a step give yourself a pat on the back and celebrate your progress as you move forward on this journey. You are one of a very few willing to take intentional action to change the direction of your life. So celebrate your courage.

One small reminder, though, is that you can only change yourself. If your dissatisfaction comes from a poor relationship, you have the opportunity to tell the person how you would like that relationship to change in an effort to improve it. I know there are some people who refuse to engage in the process and as a result, you may be left feeling dissatisfied and frustrated. In those circumstances, you have a choice to change your perspective on the situation and the person. You have the opportunity to use prayer to create a more amenable attitude in that person.

Bathe all your relationships with prayer before you begin the process. James tells us in James 5:16b, "The prayer of a righteous man is powerful and effective." Allow God to prepare their heart before you begin to engage them in crafting a better relationship. God can create a cooperative and understanding heart where there was none before.

Dear Jesus,

Thank you for giving me the Holy Spirit to guide and direct my life and teach me to be holy. Please create in me a clean heart and a right spirit within me. I desire to see people through your eyes so that I do not fall into the trap of taking your grace given each and every day but not giving it out to others. I choose not to be bankrupt spiritually. Fill me to overflowing with your Spirit so that I might be a blessing to those you put in my life. You satisfy all my desires with good things. Thank you, Jesus. Amen.

"*Do not store up for yourselves treasures on earth, where moth and rust destroy, and where thieves break in and steal. But store up for yourselves treasures in heaven, where moth and rust do not destroy, and where thieves do not break in and steal. For where your treasure is, there your heart will be also.*"

Matthew 6: 19-21

Clarifying Your Values

Have you ever wondered why certain experiences always frustrate you or cause you to get angry? Could it be that one of your values is being dishonored? Often we have our values trampled on because we haven't been able to identify our values and, thus, cannot stand up for them.

Value-based living is truly the most satisfying and peaceful way of life. What does value-based living mean to you? How does it look? To answer that, the first step is to identify your core values. You will be unpacking a step at a time the values that may be buried inside your subconscious mind.

> *Your values are your worldview or the prism through which you see the world.*

Most people have difficulty identifying three or four values that they hold dear. In reality, we each have many values in each of the areas you dealt with on the Wheel of Life. The role of values is to guide your life like an internal GPS as you make decisions each day. Your values are your worldview or the prism through which you see the world.

God created us in the image of God, *Imago Deo,* which means God placed His value system in us. If you are living in accord with your values, your values become your default mechanism for making decisions. However, if you do not even know what your values are, your default mechanism may simply be the repeat of the same behavior, even if it has always yielded negative results. Or, you procrastinate and don't make decisions or let others make them for you. God placed His values in us at our creation, but you also absorbed your parents' values into your subconscious from childhood experiences. Your parents taught you by actions or inaction. If you saw your parents handle money carelessly you may not value living within your means. If one of your parents had an affair leading to a divorce, you may not value fidelity in marriage. Often we only observed, but did not discuss those values within our families. It takes an intentional process to look deep into your soul and take out your core values and examine them.

In a life purpose class I taught, one young woman went through this exercise only to find out that she had internalized her parents' value system. She determined she no longer believed in many of those values. Yet she had allowed those values to guide her life up to that point. It became a more difficult assignment from there to discover what she believed in, having never before examined her core values.

If you cannot identify your value system, how can you know if you are living in harmony with it? What happens if you are not living in agreement with your values? Often, living out of alignment with your values, shows up in frustration, anger, unhappiness, and dissatisfaction. Have you experienced any of those feelings? Consider what value may have been dishonored in that situation; did you or did someone else dishonor your core values? For instance, you may be angry because someone close to you did not honor your "time" by coming late to a dinner date. You put forth a lot of effort for the event and they did not make being on time a priority.

When you live outside your value system, the most popular philosophy of the day or the loudest voices may sway you. In James 1:6b-8, we read, "...because he who doubts is like the wave of the sea, blown and tossed by the wind. That man should not think he will receive anything from the Lord, he is a double-minded man, unstable in all he does."

Our family has recently had some experiences with kayaks and fast moving rivers. You may not know this about kayaking, but when kayakers go under the water they do not automatically pop back up. When I have watched kayakers preparing for a race over rapids, they are so skilled they make it look like gravitational pull pops them right back up. Unfortunately, that is not what happens. It takes great skill and core strength to push them up against the gravitational pull to stay down under. If you are a novice, you could drown before you are able to bring yourself upright. I believe kayaking is an analogy for life. Picture yourself in this kayak, on a fast moving river in one of the most beautiful places in Colorado. The scenery is spectacular, the air is fresh, and the sun is shining. You seem to be floating along effortlessly until you come upon a rapid. All of a sudden, you have lost control and you are bobbing and weaving and doing everything you can to stay upright, but you eventually go

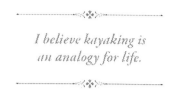

I believe kayaking is an analogy for life.

down. The key to staying upright in a kayak is core strength. It is not so different in real life. It is your core values that keep you upright and able to stay true to your values as the storms of life come at you with a vengeance. Without a clear understanding of your core values, you will sink into a miry pit of bad decisions, bouncing back and forth without a clear direction or a strong conviction about how you should handle the stormy weather. Does this describe how you are handling life?

Do you know women who cannot make decisions because they lack confidence or who repeatedly make poor decisions? The amount of energy expended in living a life without a rudder or internal compass is enormous and exhausting. They question and worry over every decision – like a teeter totter, going back and forth from one end to the other trying to keep their equilibrium.

Such women drown in worry and indecision. Does it make sense that when you have a clear standard of behavior, you are able to choose which situations to engage in and which to avoid; or would it help you veer away from situations that may compromise your values? How would that simplify your life? With many of your core values hiding in your subconscious mind, it may take some thoughtful work to uncover them. Because your belief system governs your behavior, it is extremely important to unveil your beliefs and values. Have you ever wondered why you do the things you do that get you into trouble? Check out your beliefs in that area of your life. You may find that you do not know what you believe and are being blown to and fro by the beliefs of your friends or the prevailing societal norms instead of your own core values. The following exercises will help you discover the values you hold dear.

Look at three ways in which you can begin to identify your values.

1. Some values are submerged in your subconscious[4]. To unveil them, ask this question, "What has made you angry or frustrated recently?" It is likely that it happened because the experience dishonored a value important to you. Have you ever gotten angry with someone who is always late? It could be that they were not valuing your time or you might have been angry because you value timeliness and they made you late.

   _____

   _____

   _____

   _____

2. Ask yourself this question, "What am I so overly concerned about that it makes my family crazy[5]? Family members may tease you about being somewhat fanatical about it. My husband makes lists all the time. So far he hasn't followed me around the house making lists for me, but if he did, I would put that behavior in this category. Are you so detailed-oriented that it makes your family crazy?

   _____

   _____

   _____

   _____

3. What things in your life are "must haves" or you feel unhinged[6]? For example, you may insist on putting everything in order in your home before you can leave town. Or you may insist on spending all holidays with your family.

   _____

   _____

   _____

   _____

   _____

Along with your worldview, comes a set of rules by which you live. You may never have looked at the principles with which you order your life as rules, but they are because they put boundaries on your behavior. You may make a rule to live by being a person of integrity. If that is the case, chances are you would always give back the extra change you received mistakenly from a financial transaction. You may insist on going to church every Sunday because you value your relationship with Jesus Christ and see this as a way of worshiping Him and being spiritually fed. You may live below your income level because you believe you who are blessed should give to the less fortunate. Is it beginning to make sense that rules govern your self-imposed boundaries?

This next exercise will continue the process of uncovering your values as you think of your own personal rules around which you structure your life.

Write down **10 Rules That You Live By.**[7] Ask yourself what personal rules you live by. An example may be, I believe daily Bible study is necessary to feed my soul. Another example may be that you believe in risk taking – nothing ventured, nothing gained. Or you may be committed to living below your income level and giving a portion of your income to charity. I know my mother often told me "If you cannot say anything nice, do not say anything at all." It could be that you believe education is your ticket to prosperity. It may help you to look at the messages your parents repeated so often it seemed like a broken record. Another way to discern these rules is to look at what you taught your children as life principles. It can be about relationships, money, education, family life, spiritual life, etc.

1. _____

2. _____

3. _____

4. _____

5. _____

6. _____

7. _____

8. _____

9. _____

10. _____

Another tool to help in this process is to look at five key moments in your life and list them. For example, when I got rheumatic fever as a child, it changed my life dramatically. It did affect the way I looked at life. I valued my health more than someone without that experience. It may be a divorce in the family, a death in the family or an embarrassing situation. After listing these pivotal moments in your life, answer the questions that follow.

1. _____

2. _____

3. _____

4. _____

5. _____

1. What stood out about these experiences?

   _____

   _____

   _____

2. Was what you were doing the pivotal point or was it who was there?

   _____

   _____

   _____

   _____

3. What you learned from those events may be a key to identifying your values. What values can you identify from those experiences?

_____

_____

_____

Next, is an exercise to identify a value attached to each identified rule. Whether you realize it or not, each rule is based on a value. Try to pinpoint the value upon which each rule is based in the **10 Rules to Live By.** You may base more than one rule on the same value. If that is the case, try to come up with a total of 10 values you hold dear.

1. _____

2. _____

3. _____

4. _____

5. _____

6. _____

7. _____

8. _____

9. _____

10. _____

Finally, rank these values in order of priority.

1. _____

2. _____

3. _____

4. _____

5. _____

6. _____

7. _____

8. _____

9. _____

10. _____

What did you learn or re-learn from this?

_____

_____

_____

_____

In what ways are you currently living in alignment with those identified values?

_____

_____

_____

_____

If not, what actions can you take to be more in alignment with those values?

_____

_____

_____

_____

What steps are you willing to take to live in harmony with your values?

_____

_____

_____

_____

_____

What action can you take today, next week, and next month to accomplish your goals?

_____

_____

_____

_____

_____

_____

You have made some new discoveries and had some "aha" moments through these exercises. What will you do with what you have learned? Never waste an opportunity to make new decisions based on new discoveries. We all have values, but we don't all know what they are.

Are you beginning to see the effects of being out of alignment with your values? Do you see areas where you have been ignoring your values and as a result, it has taken its toll on you? Without having well-defined values, it is easy to make decisions counter to them and then experience frustration, dissatisfaction and a general feeling of unhappiness. You are now at a place to make better decisions honoring your newly discovered values. We will move on to discovering your strengths and passions which will then put you in a good position to develop your life mission or life purpose statement. Then, the life purpose statement will guide your decision-making from here on out.

Dear Heavenly Father, you do not change like the shifting shadows. You are the rock of my salvation. Guide my every decision with your sweet spirit. May my life be a sweet fragrance to you. Help me be aware when I am not honoring the values you placed in me. Give me a course correction. Be my light in the darkness. Show me the way to live that honors your values. In Jesus name, I pray. Amen.

"It is fine to be zealous, provided the purpose is good, and to be so always and not just when I am with you."

Galatians 4:18

"Each one should use whatever gift he has received to serve others, faithfully administering God's grace in its various forms."

I Peter 4:10

Strengths and Passions

Do you see others' strengths but have difficulty in identifying and admitting your strengths? Often, I find women embarrassed to admit their strengths because it feels like bragging. Many women grew up to believe that if they talked about their strengths, they were being prideful. Is it any wonder women as a rule have difficulty accepting and verbalizing what their gifts and strengths are?

In Ephesians 2:10, the Apostle Paul encourages us with the following words, "For we are God's workmanship, created in Christ Jesus to do good works, which God prepared in advance for us to do." This passage tells us God has a plan for us to do good works for His glory. Can it be that our mighty God would give us works to do and then not equip us to do the work? I believe He has equipped each of us perfectly for the work He has ordained for us to do. God has given you the intellect, the abilities and the passion to fulfill your life purpose. Our abilities are energized through the Holy Spirit as we use them. I think we can all relate to times when we were put on a shelf for a time and then called back to service. I know when this has happened to me, my abilities are a little rusty and I needed extra preparation time to use them effectively again. This is a reason to use our abilities, intellect and passions on a continual basis rather than to hide them under a bushel where they wither.

Pride is a sin all humanity must try to avoid, but God wants us to value ourselves as people made in His image. We are to honor our abilities by using them to God's glory and blessing others as we use them. We deprive others of the blessings if we fail to use our gifts. If we spend all our time doing things outside our strength areas, we may deprive others of the opportunity to serve in their strength areas.

God has created you for greatness! To be clear, this is not so we can boast in ourselves, but to be used mightily by God for His glory. The Psalmist (8:5) says, "You made him a little lower than the heavenly beings and crowned him with glory and honor." When you think about how intricate and powerful our physical bodies are, can you imagine that God expected so little of His magnificent

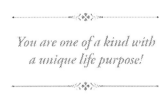

You are one of a kind with a unique life purpose!

creation? Your personality is intertwined with a multitude of traits that are unique to you. God developed a special concoction of traits just for you. No one is just like you. You are one of a kind with a unique life purpose! If you were just like someone else, one of you would be unnecessary.

How can you live your life purpose if you do not know your unique strengths and passions? The goal of this chapter is to enable you to recognize your strengths and your passions to allow you to live in that sweet spot more often called your *strength zone*.

Strengths and passions can be differentiated from acquired skills, in that acquired skills require practice and may not be high on your list of enjoyable tasks. As we change positions within our chosen field or change careers, each position offers us opportunities to acquire new skills. Here is an illustration of the difference between operating mostly in your strength areas versus your acquired skills areas. Picture a steel ladder leading up to the diving board. The ladder is symbolic of your strength areas. The diving board, which is flexible, has a lot of possible movement up and down. This represents your acquired skills. When you operate in your strength areas, you feel more secure and enjoy your job more robustly.

The strength and stability of the steel ladder represents the enthusiasm and self-assurance you exhibit when operating in your strength areas. When you operate mostly in your acquired skills area, you are literally on the edge of the diving board, feeling overwhelmed, frustrated and about to fall off the edge into dissatisfaction and apathy.

Your acquired skills do not give you the energy needed to sustain an enthusiastic view of the workplace and the job at hand. It is important to differentiate between acquired skills and strength areas to ensure you look for opportunities to use your strengths more often and, perhaps, delegate the activities in your acquired skill areas. You will be amazed how much more innovative and enthusiastic you will be at work. Much of the energy that was being used up in your acquired skill areas will be released.

Now, to identify strengths, think back to your childhood. You may have recognized talents or interests that differed from your siblings. You may have noticed one of your siblings was drawn to reading while another was more attracted to sports. Passions and strengths have a gravitational pull. Another way to distinguish strengths and passions is to look at those things you can do for hours and not realize how much time has passed. Some people are passionate about their mission and work tirelessly at it without pay. They jump over, around or through the obstacles. That is passion!

Look at things at which you excel but you notice others find difficult. Writing is easy for me, but it takes more time for my husband to formulate his ideas. However, he is a better editor than I. Some people are great with balancing checkbooks or working with numbers because it comes easily to them. We don't often think of Emotional Intelligence Quotient (EQ) when we look at strengths, but it is as important as Intellectual Intelligence Quotient (IQ). EQ is the ability to get along with people, listen to people, negotiate, or bring consensus from diverse thoughts. All are ways to manage people.

Henri Matisse, in contrast to Picasso, did not have a yearning or a compulsion to paint. His interest began when his mother brought him paints in young adulthood to cheer him up after a bout of illness. He soon found painting was easy for him. He then refined his talent through how to paint books[8]. In my own family, my children all played basketball but only one of them had it come easily to them. If the other three had spent an equal amount of time playing the game, they still would not have performed as well as the one for whom it came easily. There was no passion involved just rapid learning.

Can you think of times when you act spontaneously, without forethought? Something just spills out of you. This is a clue to a strength or passion. For example, do you know someone who walks into an event and sees there is no order, only chaos? They immediately move in to organize what previously was an out of control event. Or, when you see someone hurt, you rush over to help them out without any thought of how you might be affected. At the same time, others may take time to assess the situation and the risk they may be taking before they act. You may be one who is always able to come up with an appropriate joke to match the situation. It is not something you have to think about, it just comes to you and you share it. Can you recognize in yourself the tendency to act spontaneously in certain situations?

_____

_____

_____

1. What longing can you identify from childhood? It usually feels like an internal urging or tugging. For example, Matt Damon and Ben Affleck, from the time they were in grade school, loved to act.[10] Your passions and strengths may draw you to care for pets or promote healthy living. You may rearrange your furniture often because you have an eye for design and decorating.

    _____

    _____

    _____

    _____

2. In what ways do you find gratification in doing a certain activity?[11] That is a key to discovering your strengths and passions. Your brain has a way of creating good feelings when you do something in your strength areas. I am drawn to encouraging people to move toward their best self by coaching, encouraging and teaching them. I also feel gratified if I have had an impact on getting legislation passed. You may find great fulfillment in cooking and baking, planning meals or parties or designing landscaping.

    _____

    _____

    _____

    _____

Here are other questions you can ask yourself to help you discover your strengths:

3. What activity or situation pulls you in? For me, it can be advocating for children and families or helping people become healthy. Do you like challenges related to finances, puzzles, solving problems with people or things? Do you find humor in every situation? Does your heart lean toward caring for animals? Do you love to be around children?

    _____

    _____

    _____

    _____

4. At what do you excel that your friends find very difficult[12]? I can operate in an environment of chaos and focus where others cannot. Can you size up a problem quickly? Can you take charge of a situation easily? Can you foresee the possible obstacles? Do you have an uncanny ability to see what spice is missing in a dish you are making?

    _____

    _____

    _____

    _____

5. List your passions and strengths as you now see them.

    _____

    _____

    _____

    _____

I love this prayer from Ephesians 1:19-21a, "I pray also that the eyes of your heart may be enlightened in order that you may know the hope to which he has called you, the riches of his glorious inheritance in the saints, and his incomparably great power for us who believe. That power is like the working of his mighty strength, which he exerted in Christ when he raised him from the dead and seated him at his right hand in the heavenly realms."

God has given us great power as co-heirs with Christ to be all we are meant to be. Anything you come upon as struggles will not exceed the power that raised Christ from the dead. You are equipped for every situation. Call on the power of the Spirit to equip you with courage to live the abundant life God so desires you to have.

Do you now feel you have identified your areas of strength? If you would like to confirm those strengths, try the following websites. I recommend you do the work first. Then take the strengths inventory as confirmation of what you have discovered on your own. The free website is: www.authentichappiness.com. The site offers several different inventories. I recommend the 240 question strength survey. Another resource is the book *"Now, Discover Your Strengths"* by Marcus Buckingham and Donald O. Clifton, Ph.D. Their website is the following: www.strengthsfinder.com. You can access the Strengths Finder Inventory by buying their book which gives you a code to access the test online.

Dear Heavenly Father, you put in my DNA unique strengths that you chose for me for your purposes. Help me to identify those strengths and build my confidence to use those strengths in the paths you will open up for me during this discovery process. Speak to my heart about what direction you want me to go. Amen.

"A longing fulfilled is sweet to the soul," Proverbs 13:19a

"He fulfills the desires of those who fear him; he hears their cry and saves them." Psalm 145:19

Develop a Life Purpose or Mission Statement

There is no shortage of good works you could be doing with your time, but are they things God has called you to do? We can have the life drained out of us by saying "yes" to good works to which God has not called us, when, in essence, those activities prevent us from being available for the good works God has ordained us to do.

There is no shortage of good works you could be doing with your time, but are they things God has called you to do?

I am not often mistaken for a Martha Stewart or a Betty Crocker type, unlike most of the women in my family. I am the odd duck of the group as I look at it now. I cringe when I am called to bake or cook for others because I don't enjoy doing either. Just so you don't feel too sorry for my husband, I do cook almost every night, but it is not something I gain any satisfaction from nor do I enjoy it. Consequently, I spend little time shoring up my skills in that area. My Standard Operating Procedure (S.O.P.) these days is that I try something new when I have company for dessert. I plan to make two desserts, the first one which is new to me and the second is in case the first fails. My husband has watched this S.O.P. for so long all he wants me to do is buy a dessert. He just doesn't understand women. Actually, one of my strengths is courage and adventure, I just haven't thought of it in the kitchen. Cooking is not in my strength zone, can you tell?

Living in harmony with your values, strengths and passions is the ultimate in living a fulfilled life. It is a feeling of being whole, complete. How differently would your lives look if you were living in harmony with your values, strengths and passions? You were not made to be ordinary. To believe that all I have to do is look at our intricate bodies. God's design for our bodies is so amazing. Did you know that our bodies are made up of tiny but powerful individual cells with each having enough information to fill 1,000 sets of encyclopedias[13]. This is beyond my comprehension. My brain just has no capacity to comprehend all the intricacies of our bodies. If you doubt you were made to make a significant difference in the world, ask God to help you see what that means for you. Then repeat the prayer of the centurion from Mark 9:24, "I do believe; help me overcome my unbelief."

John Maxwell (2007), internationally known authority on leadership, and well-known pastor and speaker, in his book, *Talent Is Never Enough*, said the secret to his passion is[14]:

1. I am gifted at what I do. (Strength zone)

2. What I do makes a difference. (Results)

3. When I do what I was made to do, I feel most alive. (Purpose)

A person without a purpose is like a dog chasing his tail. He never gets anywhere. Another way of looking at this is having no sense of direction. I personally have no sense of direction when I travel outside my hometown. I know first-hand the confusion and chaos created by lacking a sense of where you are or where you are going. It is painful, scary and exhausting.

A person without a purpose is like a dog chasing his tail. He never gets anywhere.

When you are clueless as to your life purpose, the life you are living may not be your authentic life. You were made to serve others, but each of you has a different arena. As you search for your purpose, you may want to read the book, *Outlive Your Life* (2010) by Max Lucado. He gives you ample ideas of how to reach out to others less fortunate than you. You may find you are passionate about philanthropic endeavors.

Coach Dale Brown in his book, *Words To Lift Your Spirits*, said "Faith, belief and conviction are the keys, the spurs, and loud alarm that will wake up the sleeping giant within all of us[15]." Are you ready to awaken the sleeping giant within you? You must believe you have at least one specific purpose for your life to have the energy it takes to uncover your

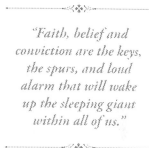

"Faith, belief and conviction are the keys, the spurs, and loud alarm that will wake up the sleeping giant within all of us."

purpose and then intentionally live it out. Some of you, like me, may be passionate about a number of different things.

Before you work specifically on your life purpose, you are going to have the opportunity to write your future life script. Do you believe you are currently living a life script written by you or by someone else, like a parent, a spouse, or a sibling? If you are, what is it like living a script written by someone other than you? Today, you have the opportunity to create your own script for your future life. This will be unique to you! It is the life you desire to live – planting that perennial garden I mentioned earlier in this book.

You have now identified your values, your strengths and your passions. It is time to put all of those elements into your life script. Visualize yourself on a stage talking to a crowd sharing your passions. What would you be telling these people about your passion and how you are living it out? It is important not to allow self-limiting beliefs rob you of your ability to dream big. Self-limiting beliefs speak lies to your mind and heart. The lies Satan tells you are that you are either too stupid, not pretty enough, too overweight, or too old, etc. When they rear their ugly head, discard the thought and replace it with a positive "I can do it". This doesn't happen overnight, it takes practice to turn a negative statement into a positive statement. We will talk more about this in the chapter on Overcoming Obstacles.

Exercise: If someone were to make a movie of your life featuring the next three to five years, what would it look like? Dream big and do not let money, age or time limit you. Your assignment is to write a life script looking forward three to five years. This is a script that does not include self-limiting beliefs which discourage dreaming big. Be sure to honor your strengths, passions and values. If for some reason, you cannot think that far in advance, begin with six months and gradually fan out to three to five years. Robert Browning has said, "My business is not to remake myself but make the absolute best of what God has made."

> *Robert Browning has said, "My business is not to remake myself but make the absolute best of what God has made."*

_____

_____

_____

_____

_____

_____

_____

1. What did you learn or re-learn from this experience?

    _____

    _____

    _____

    _____

    _____

2. What changes did your heart and mind go through as you wrote your future life script?

    _____

    _____

    _____

    _____

    _____

3. To what degree did you believe it is possible for you to achieve what you have written in your life script?

    _____

    _____

    _____

    _____

4. In what ways were your values, strengths and passions represented in your life script?

_____

_____

_____

_____

_____

5. What benefit will you receive if you are successful?

_____

_____

_____

_____

_____

_____

Were you able to identify whether you have been living a life script written by someone else? If so, it must have felt very empowering to now write your *own* future script. It would have felt like a burden was lifted. There is great energy when you are doing what gives you great satisfaction. What will you do today to move yourself in that direction?

Now that you have written a script for your future self, begin to think about your life purpose or mission in life. This should be a great starting point for you to begin to define what you were made to do with your life.

To begin, remind yourself of things in which you excel, what others say your talents are, and what yearnings you have that draws you like a lure draws a fish to the bait. You are drawn to certain behaviors and activities. I happen to be very passionate about protecting the Christian principles upon which this nation was founded. I am drawn to those discussions and to activities that further that goal. I am also passionate about helping people improve their health by losing weight in order for them to be able to realize their dreams. As you analyze your interest areas, key words in your core values and strengths will begin to form phrases and then sentences related to your life purpose. I don't want you to think this is easy for most people to do because it is not.

If you haven't come to a point where you are able to identify your passions and life purpose, take some time before you move on to think about this. You are not on a time schedule. Sometimes the awareness does not come right away. Once you are able to formulate a life purpose statement, you may find that you will tweak it every year to reflect what new understanding you have received.

Exercise: Write sample life purpose statements until you feel you have hit on yours in 15 or fewer words. For example, one of my life purposes is: empowering people to fulfill their God-given life purpose through the process of teaching and coaching. Metaphorically speaking, I am a catalyst to move people forward.

1. What feelings were ignited by writing your mission statement?

   _____

   _____

   _____

   _____

2. What benefit did you receive from this exercise?

   _____

   _____

   _____

   _____

3. How does your mission statement encompass your values, strengths and passions?

   _____

   _____

   _____

   _____

4. Based on your stated life purpose, are you living in alignment with your life purpose today?

   _____

   _____

   _____

   _____

5. What actions can you take today to move toward your purpose? Which ones will you commit to doing?

   _____

   _____

   _____

   _____

6. What will you do this week, this month, this year to incrementally move you toward your life purpose?

_____

_____

_____

_____

What you are doing in this book is learning to use the tools I am giving you to further pursue your life purpose. I want to encourage you to keep asking yourself questions as you peel back one layer at a time. You need to know that some layers take more time than others. Remember this is a process that happens over time and not on command. Take whatever time you need to be in thought and solitude to ponder what God has created you to do. Then, pray for eyes to see and a heart to understand what God has planted in you, the pearl of great value, to share with the world. He has great adventures in store for you if you will only ask for His leading.

Dear Abba Father,

When you created me, you had in mind a purpose for my life. You placed in me these passions and strengths. Please open my eyes to see that purpose. Help me overcome my unbelief in any area that is keeping me from fulfilling my life purpose. I lean on your gentle guidance. Your ways are perfect, LORD. Prepare the way and I will follow. In the powerful name of Jesus, I pray, Amen.

"Finally, brothers, whatever is true, whatever is noble, whatever is right, whatever is pure, whatever is lovely, whatever is admirable- if anything is excellent or praiseworthy-think about such things."

Philippians 4:8

Overcoming Obstacles

If we think there will come a time when obstacles in life will finally just disappear because we have finally arrived, we are fooling ourselves. As long as there are people in our world, all who are imperfect, there will be sin, obstacles and trials. In John 16:33, Jesus tells us, "I have told you these things, so that in me you may have peace. In this world you will have trouble. But take heart! I have overcome the world." I hope that comforts you. There is nothing that can overcome us if we are in Christ, feeding on His Word.

What we do not realize is that frequently we give greater weight to the obstacles that come at us externally than those that come from within. Do you remember the principle that what we believe governs what we do? Can you think of a time when you talked yourself out of doing something you really wanted to do because of self-doubt?

Take a minute and consider some ways you self-sabotage by what you think. Anyone who has ever gone on a diet knows full well we have an amazing ability to self-sabotage by what we tell ourselves. Then we fail. I have been on many of the popular diets. My struggle with weight began when I was in seventh grade and went into the hospital with pneumonia and left with rheumatic fever. I was sent home to be tutored my seventh grade year. I was not allowed to exercise for the next five years. So what else is there to do but watch soap operas and eat? As soon as I felt strong enough to begin exercising by walking home from school and work, I did. Then I began to lose weight. By then, however,

I had developed some bad habits. I tended to be a chocoholic. I am not a very tall person so every pound shows. In adulthood, I have stayed within 25 lbs. of my adult weight, mostly at the lesser end of that scale, but only because I work at it. I have finally found a way of life and lifestyle change that works well for me. I find I need a lot of protein to stave off cravings and hunger. So I have found a nutritional program of maintenance that works well for me. But I remember all the lies I told myself. I would say, "I'll never have the discipline to be successful" or "I will just cheat today. One time won't matter." Can you relate? We also fool ourselves by conveniently forgetting what we've eaten that day which sabotages our efforts in dieting. We choose not to create a food journal for fear of what we will find out.

In much the same way, people do not write down their goals because they do not want to see that they failed to achieve them. When in reality, if you write them down and do not achieve them, you at least can see if you have moved forward. Then you can re-strategize and set new goals with new timelines and there is no disgrace in that.

Think of your attitudes as potential "enemies from within" which Jim Rohn[16], America's great business philosopher, mentioned in his recorded lectures. Have you ever given up pursuing a goal because of the following attitudes?

- *Discouragement* – Some people in your life are firefighters,[17] who will throw cold water on the fire of passion that burns within you. Try to guard the amount of time you spend with firefighters until you are strong enough in your desire to withstand their negativism.
- *Indifference* – Your desire is squelched because you believe whatever you do will not make a difference.
- *Indecision* – You are without a barometer to help you make a decision.
- *Doubt* – You are not convinced you can pull it off or think Murphy's Law will certainly come into play somehow. Satan's lies infiltrate your mind.
- *Worry* – You are not able to overcome your fears.
- *Over-caution* – Fear of what you might encounter is so strong and so you do nothing.
- *Pessimism* – Satan's lies about your inadequacy permeates your mind.

There are other "enemies from within", for instance, self-limiting beliefs we have harbored. I mentioned self-limiting beliefs in the last chapter. A self-limiting belief is feeling inadequate to reach your goals. It is a belief that says because I am "not smart enough" or "young enough" or "pretty enough" to accomplish my goals, I am not even going to try.

Myths we have believed from childhood may have derailed our goals as well. These myths may be things your significant others have said about you or things you have inferred from experiences you had as a child. Identify your self-limiting beliefs and the myths to see if there is any evidence that they are true today. If there is no evidence that these beliefs are true, discard them and begin to believe that you are able.

Negative self-talk is probably the most pernicious of all the "enemies from within". Negative self-talk is evil because it dishonors God's creation - you. It is a poison to our souls. The source is Satan's lies. His goal is to make us as ineffective as possible. He does not want us to be used by God. Many people will not put themselves out there to make a change or to make a difference in the world because Satan's accusations come with a vengeance. He wins this battle unless we use who we are in Christ to combat his lies.

Negative self-talk is probably the most pernicious of all the "enemies from within".

Our minds think thoughts so much faster than our mouth can speak them. Your mind is constantly saying things to you either in pictures or words. Stoop[18] found we speak 150-200 words per minute, but he found that some research indicates our thoughts race at 1300 words per minute. Think of your brain as a movie that runs 24/7 with pictures, words and feelings. For example, think of a time you were in a lecture or listening to a sermon, while at the same time thinking of your grocery list. The mind is the ultimate in multi-tasking. The mind is a wonderful thing when used for good.

When your self-esteem is at a low, remind yourself who you are in Christ. There is nothing more affirming than that. Repeat the attributes you were given as a child of God, "I am adopted, blessed, forgiven, loved, righteous and a new creation." Practice saying this aloud at first and then repeat those affirmations in your mind. How does it feel to hear positive statements after having heard the negative for so long? Empowering, right? The more you say these positive statements, the more positive your thoughts will become. The Bible is filled with encouraging words which you can repeat and fill your minds with the good news about who you are in Christ. God loves to hear His words spoken aloud. There is power in speaking God's Word and it is a shield against Satan.

How do you stop the negative self-talk when it comes with such force and frequency? Can you think of a strategy to turn your negative self-talk into a positive, affirming statement about you? It begins with recognizing when it is happening. For instance, you want to go back to school. In your head you are hearing, "I am too old" or "things have changed so much, I probably wouldn't succeed" or "it is not cost effective for me to go because I can not make enough money to pay back the cost of my education." Begin to retrain your brain to find positive, affirming words to counter the negative. For instance, begin saying, "I am able to go to school and be successful. I learn new things everyday. I may not know what the future will bring, but learning is always a good thing."

None of us want to face obstacles and then fail. It is human nature to want to avoid pain and failure. It is not until we are on the other side of the pain and failure that we realize the personal growth and the empowerment gained by overcoming and persevering through a storm. Each trial is an opportunity for growth. Can you imagine what we would have missed in innovation if Thomas Edison had given up after his 5,999th attempt to find an adequate filament for his light bulb just before his success on his 6,000th attempt? Each failure is one step closer to success. Just think what Edison learned about the 5,999 products that did not work for the light bulb but could be used for other inventions.

Obstacles that other people put in our way can be formidable but less so than those we put in our own way. They, however, can be opportunities to create a new perspective or a challenge to walk over, around or through the obstacle. In one of my life purpose classes, there was a woman who exhibited what is possible in the human spirit when someone is highly motivated. She suffered from a very painful bone disease. This woman was in intense pain all the time and as a result, she could not walk. Her story is one of heroic proportions. Despite the objections of her family, she came to class because it lifted her spirits to be in class with intelligent women in a stimulating learning environment. Determined to be in class each week, she displayed the overwhelming energy available to us when we have a goal. She became the hero of the class because she was overcoming huge obstacles each week as she struggled to get to class. No other person in the class had an obstacle that could mirror what she overcame each week. If you believe you have overwhelming obstacles in your path, remember this courageous lady and know you can overcome your obstacles as well.

One of the most debilitating obstacles we all face at one time or another is to feel unworthy to be loved or cared for. God created you with value. You were valuable enough for God to create a path for redemption from the beginning of time with the precious sacrifice of His only Son. God knew our free choice would lead to selfishness and sinfulness. Our value comes from God who created us and loved us while we were rebellious, stubborn sinners. God loved us before we loved Him.

Dr. Viktor Frankl, famous neurologist and psychiatrist, learned from living in the German concentration camps that attitude was often the difference between life and death. He said "Everything can be taken from us but the last of the human freedoms—to choose one's attitude in any given set of circumstances, to choose one's own way [19]".

Isn't God great? He opted not to make us mind-numbing robots, but a people with free will to choose our actions and our attitudes about our circumstances. I know that I do not always model godliness in the attitudes I choose about my circumstances. I have learned through my own bad choices as I am sure you have. If someone living in a concentration camp can take captive his thoughts and find a positive perspective, how much more are you capable of taking your thoughts captive? Paul tells us in II Corinthians 10: 4-5, "The weapons we fight with are not the weapons of the world. On the contrary, they have divine power to demolish strongholds. We demolish arguments and every pretension that sets itself up against the knowledge of God, and we take captive every thought to make it obedient to Christ."

1. What "enemies within" have you used to defeat yourself?

    _____

    _____

    _____

    _____

    _____

2. What can you do to prevent these attitudes from stealing your joy, your desire to move forward in your life journey?

    _____

    _____

    _____

    _____

    _____

3. What lies have you believed?

    _____

    _____

    _____

    _____

    _____

4. What is the source of your self-limiting beliefs? Can you prove they are true? Examine them and discard them if there is no evidence to support them. Now write an affirmative statement reversing that former belief. If you believe you are not smart enough; you re- word it to say "I am smart enough to do this thing I want to do."

    _____

    _____

    _____

    _____

    _____

5. Share with God your self-limiting belief and let God speak His truth to you in the form of a prayer to abolish the lie.

_____

_____

_____

_____

_____

Your attitudes have a profound influence on what you accomplish. Your attitudes are not forced upon you by your circumstances but are intentional decisions you make about your circumstances. Current events are frequently colored by previous negative experiences with a person or situation. Look at how that works through what is called an "Inference Ladder"[20].

An "Inference Ladder" describes how you allow yourselves to believe that your perspective is the only perspective there is in a given circumstance. It was originally believed to be created by Chris Argyris. Picture yourself building a ladder, one rung at a time.

1. You have an experience.

2. You decide "what" out of that experience you will pay attention to.

3. You assign a value to the parts of the experience you want to pay attention to which generally is influenced by your hot buttons, feelings of inadequacy, etc.

4. You assign a motive to the person who was involved in this experience.

5. You make conclusions on your attitude about their motive.

6. You are now ready to formulate a solid belief about the experience and the person.

7. You take an action in relation to that belief.

You have now determined what happened, why it happened, and what you are going to do about it. Then you act on your own preconceived ideas about the experience without ever checking out with the person involved in the situation to see if your perceptions were the least bit accurate.

Can you see how making assumptions without checking the veracity with the people involved could seriously tarnish a relationship? Consider the following experience I had dealing with wrong assumptions. I went to a dinner with friends. I walked up to a small group chatting with each other. One member of the group who is usually very friendly and eager to talk with me, this time totally ignored me. Because of a previous experience in which I thought I had disappointed my friend by what I had done, I attributed her ignoring me to that event. I did not take into consideration what she had on her plate that night. She was giving a speech and may have been feeling nervous about it. Instead, I, in one felt swoop, determined she was mad at me because of the previous experience. I did not give her the benefit of a doubt and could have decided to get angry and take an equally negative action which could have ruined a precious relationship.

You and I would benefit by taking the opportunity to push the pause button, step back from the situation, walk back down the ladder, one rung at a time to consider other possible reasons for why this event happened, giving the person the benefit of a doubt instead of nailing them to the cross for what you determined their motive to be. I have been down this bunny trail too many times, only to find out I was completely wrong about what took place and why.

Look at other more positive reasons for the experience that may have nothing to do with you at all. It could be that the person may have been dealing with their own problems which had nothing to do with you. If you check it out with the person before you get angry, hurt or disappointed in them, you may avoid a lot of unnecessary pain and anger for both of you.

Have an attitude of curiosity toward that person and ask questions to try to clear up the misunderstanding. An attitude of curiosity creates a kinder level of questioning. You cannot lose sight of the fact that in all circumstances you choose your attitude. You may be attributing previous bad experiences with a person to this new experience and the current experience may have nothing to do with the previous experience.

Keep in mind if two people are involved in a situation, there are at least two different perspectives operating. Much of our rush to judgment has to do with our own insecurities. Our perspective then is to remember our worth in God's eyes. In the end, God's eyes are the only ones that count. His love for us is empowering and gives us the strength to handle the fact that not everyone is going to always like us. He accepts our mistakes and gives us an infinite number of second chances. Can we give ourselves that same grace and others, too?

Time and again, we reinforce self-limiting beliefs about ourselves, by believing that we experienced the offensive event because we are not likable or worthy of their friendship. Take these situations into a time of prayer to let God change your perspective on the situation and let Him reassure you it is not that you are not likable or unworthy.

Dear Lord Jesus,

You know what we are thinking before the thought leaves our mouth. Help me starve my critical spirit. Help me to give more grace to people who I am feeling have offended me. You are my strength. In You, I have the strength to change my perspective to give grace to others as you give to me daily. Remind me to bring my hurt feelings to you rather than to react in hurtful ways. Help me choose to love people even those who have acted unkindly to me. In the power of Jesus name, I pray, Amen.

"Your word is a lamp to my feet and a light for my path".

Psalm 119:105

Goals and Building a Roadmap

We are on our final stop in this journey to living intentionally! The last piece of clothing in your suitcase is going to be unpacked. I pray you are beginning to believe in your ability to become a person of significance in your sphere of influence. I would have no greater joy than to see you live out your life purpose with the power of Christ in you! In Psalm 8, David reminds us that God made us a little lower than the heavenly beings and crowned us with glory and honor. Will you choose to believe that God has an awesome plan for your life and desires to have you lead a life of great significance? Jeremiah 29:11 is one of my favorite verses, he says, "For I know the plans I have for you", declares the LORD, "plans to prosper you and not to harm you, plans to give you hope and a future." God does not make promises He doesn't keep. God is the promise maker and the promise keeper. Humans cannot always be trusted to keep their promises, but thankfully, God's promises are trustworthy.

In writing your life script, you identified your desires for the near future, a direction and at least one goal. With that information you are now in a position to create concrete action steps to achieve your goals. Specific ideas lead us to action; whereas, vague ideas are a dead end.

Before you proceed to create action steps, there is another tool you will want to have in your tool box and that is discovering your motivation style. This will be important as you build a road map because it will help you build an effective accountability system.

Tamara Lowe (2009), author of *Get Motivated*, found through decades of research that most people's motivation styles fall within six categories. Lowe uses the acronym DNA to describe motivation styles as follows: Drives, Needs and Awards.

Each category has two options. In the area of Drives, you are either a Producer (P) or a Connector (C)[21]. If you are a producer, you are driven to produce or take actions which get results. If, on the other hand, you are a connector, you are motivated by relationships. In the area of Needs, you are either motivated by Stability (S) or Variety (V)[22]. Someone motivated by stability may prefer routines and familiarity because it gives one a sense of security. That feeling of security, then, motivates you. Those who are motivated by variety enjoy the fact that things change often. This person loves the challenge of flexibility at work. Awards can either be External (E) or Internal (I)[23]. Examples of external awards are monetary in nature or career advancement. Internal awards consist of verbal appreciation for the contribution one makes to the organization. I tend to be a PVI or PVE which means I am a producer who is motivated by variety and can be motivated either by monetary awards or verbal appreciation depending on the project.

If you are creating an accountability system, does it make sense that you would want to incorporate ways to motivate yourself to stay on track? Some of you will be motivated by connection. You will find you prefer some meaningful conversation before you begin work because you value relationships. It is important to know who you are working with and what is going on in their life as well as sharing what is going on in your life. You love the give and take of meaningful conversation.

You and I may have to adjust our motivation style if we were to work together successfully. For instance, I would need to take the time to talk with you about your personal life before I expected you to get down to the work at hand, since connection spurs your motivation. You, on the other hand, may need to shorten the conversation time and get down to business more quickly than is normally comfortable for you. Lowe calls this adaptation "gene splicing"[24] because you take on characteristics of the other person's motivation style in order to have a more productive collaboration.

She found that we are hardwired with our own unique motivation style in our DNA. Lowe also found what motivates one person, demotivates someone else[25]. If your path to your life purpose requires the help of someone else, you may be in a situation where you need to know not only your style of motivation but that person's as well. How many of you married a spouse with the opposite motivation style? That makes life interesting doesn't it? But can you see the value of knowing your spouse's motivation style as you seek a more meaningful life together?

Connectors are motivated by relationships. If this describes you, think of a time you were de-motivated by a situation and think of how you would turn that around to create a situation where you were motivated to act.

_____

_____

_____

_____

_____

_____

_____

_____

Producers are motivated by accomplishing projects or seeing concrete results. If you are a producer, think of a situation where you were de-motivated and turn it around to create a situation in which you are motivated to act.

_____

_____

_____

_____

_____

_____

If you prefer variety over stability, how can you arrange to have variety in your roadmap to motivate you?

_____

_____

_____

_____

_____

If you prefer stability over variety, what can you incorporate into your roadmap to encourage you to act?

_____

_____

_____

_____

_____

I am de-motivated by detail, routine and by having tight controls over me as I work on a project. I like the freedom to complete the project as I see fit. Some of you are de-motivated by too little structure in the workplace and too much flexibility. Routines give you a level of security and comfort that variety doesn't provide for you. If you are unsure what your motivational DNA is, Tamara Lowe's free website: www.GetMotivatedBook.com offers you the opportunity to take an assessment that will help you identify your motivation style. It will serve you well in personal relationships as well in the work place to know your motivational style.

You are now ready to begin creating a road map to reach your goals. Once the goal is clear, you will be ready to create concrete steps to get you there.

1. What would happen if your goals and your steps to attain those goals were vague?

    _____

    _____

    _____

2. What would happen if you lacked a time frame for accomplishing them?

    _____

    _____

    _____

Without specific goals and timelines with which to accomplish those goals, you are clueless as to how to move forward. For example, if you were taking a trip with no specific destination in mind, how would you know you had reached your destination? Exactly! You wouldn't. Does this capture for you the importance of clarity of the goal and time frame for accomplishing the goal? Do you know people who talk about wanting change but never define what that change looks like? Do they go anywhere? In my experience the answer is no. I found those people who operate this way have difficulty making decisions and are never completely comfortable with the decisions they do make.

Having a time frame creates an accountability system and gives you a measuring tool to show you have moved from Point A to Point B. If you do not reach your goal in the time specified, you go back to the drawing board and create new timelines.

It is important to have specific and measurable goals, without which you would go nowhere. And so it is with the steps in the roadmap, they must also be S.M.A.R.T.[26] steps, that is, they must be Specific, Measurable, Attainable, Relevant and Time bound. To illustrate this, if I say I want to learn to live within my financial means I would do the following. The first specific step I could take would be to create a financial journal detailing where every penny of my paycheck goes. The next step could be deciding what two things I will not buy during my next pay period. The third measurable step could be to create a budget where every penny is accounted for beginning the next full pay period.

Does this make sense? Each step was specific, measurable, attainable, relevant and given a time limit to accomplish it.

How much time have you spent actually planning your life? Most people just let life happen to them and so they react to life instead of systematically planning their lives. If you have not planned your life thus far, think how different it would have been if you had. By now, you have done a tremendous amount of work to get to this point in your journey. It takes a lot of critical thinking and discovery of what may have been buried within your subconscious. Change is scary! A fear of the unknown prevents many people from moving forward to become their authentic self. What will you do with what you have discovered? To help you decide, take some time to answer the following questions.

3. What goals did you identify in your life script?

_____

_____

_____

_____

_____

4. Which ones are of greater priority?

_____

_____

_____

_____

5. What can you do today to take a step in that direction?

_____

_____

_____

_____

6. What further information do you need to move forward?

    _____

    _____

    _____

    _____

    _____

    _____

7. What resources can help you get the answers to the questions you have or who can team up with you to accomplish your goals?

    _____

    _____

    _____

    _____

    _____

    _____

8. What can you do to build in an accountability system that keeps you on target?

    _____

    _____

    _____

    _____

    _____

9. What benchmarks can you set up to know you are moving forward in a timely fashion?

    _____

    _____

    _____

    _____

    _____

10. If you do not meet those benchmarks, how will you re-adjust your strategy to keep moving forward?

_____

_____

_____

_____

_____

11. How will you incorporate your spiritual journey with your personal journey?

_____

_____

_____

_____

_____

You have identified your motivation style and your goals which you have created to be in alignment with your life purpose. Each time you identify a new goal, you can take the same SMART steps outlined in this chapter to help you develop a roadmap to the new goal. You have a blueprint for implementing the changes you are bound to experience over time. My prayer for you is to never stop learning about your authentic self and to allow God to move you in new directions in His timing. God doesn't consider our comfort as a goal for His children. I pray you will not fear change but embrace it as God opens new doors for you. You have taken quite a journey with me. Use these tools to craft a more purposeful life for yourself. You no longer need to feel lost and insignificant. I pray you will continue to review what you learned about yourself on this journey to refine your path to be more in harmony with your values, strengths and passions. Live intentionally for what God cherishes – adding value to people, in other words, loving people! With specific goals utilizing your strengths and passions, life will be an adventure every day to see how God will use you to accomplish His goals for you. We each have a function and a purpose in the Body of Christ and the world becomes a better place as we fulfill our God-given purpose.

I am so proud of you for taking this journey with me. You may not realize this, but you are one of a very few who have the courage to complete this process of self-discovery. I am sure at some point in this process you were not always comfortable. You are not the same person who picked up this book and began to read it. You have taken some risks and done some things you have never done before. How does it feel? Change can be very uncomfortable not only for you but those you live with. Once you have moved toward transforming your life in some area, you relate differently to those people close to you and they notice. Sometimes it makes them uncomfortable and they may resist your positive changes. Do not be discouraged. They are experiencing a loss of the previous relationship, in essence, grieving over what was. They will survive but it will take them time to mourn the lost relationship. Allow them time to adjust. Pray together. Allow time for them to accept your changes.

As you search for ways to use your strengths and passions to influence your world, it may be helpful to know what John Maxwell said, "One is too small a number for greatness".[27] God is waiting in the wings to help you accomplish great things for Him. You can combine your efforts with other like-minded individuals and conquer greater feats. Your path may not be one you need to go alone.

> *John Maxwell said,*
> *"One is too small a*
> *number for greatness".*

I want to encourage you to continue on this path of transformation. It is an ongoing process until we meet Jesus face to face. You will always need to tweak your life purpose statement to allow for new knowledge, new discoveries and new experiences that come your way. I look forward to hearing about your personal life purpose journey. Go forward onto a life of significance and purpose with God leading the way!

"A pearl which has reached maturity is released by the oyster to be enjoyed by the world for its beauty."

You have been refined through the sands of life to become your God-given pearl. Go and share your intellect, your strengths and your passions with those God has placed in your path. Live intentionally and authentically!

"Shout for joy to the LORD, all the earth. Worship the LORD with gladness; come before him with joyful songs. Know that the LORD is God. It is he who made us, and we are his; we are his people, the sheep of his pasture. Enter his gates with thanksgiving and his courts with praise; give thanks to him and praise his name. For the LORD is good and his love endures forever; his faithfulness continues through all generations." Psalm 100: 1-5

You are a precious gift to the world. As a Christian, you are:
Adopted into God's family – Eph. 1:5
Blessed-Psalm 40:4, 84:5, 112:1
Co-heirs with Christ-Galatians 4:7
Delivered from the penalty of sin which is death- Romans 6:23
Eternally to live with Christ-John 3:16
Forgiven-John 1:9
Given a new identity in Christ-2 Corinthians 5:17
Heaven bound-Philippians 3:20

Additional Resources

Marcus A. Buckingham and Clifton, Donald O., *Now, Discover Your Strengths* (New York: The Free Press, 2001).

Todd Duncan, *The Power To Be Your Best* (Nashville, TN: The W Publishing Group a Division of Thomas Nelson, Inc., 1999).

Tamara Lowe, *Get Motivated* (New York: Doubleday, 2009).

Max Lucado, *Outlive Your Life* (Nashville, TN: Thomas Nelson, Inc., 2010).

John Maxwell, *Talent Is Never Enough* (Nashville, TN: Thomas Nelson, Inc., 2007).

John Ortberg, *If You Want To Walk On Water, You've Got To Get Out Of The Boat* (Grand Rapids, MI: Zondervan Publishing House, 2001).

www.authentichappiness.com – take VIA Strengths Survey – free
www.getmotivatedbook.com - take a free survey on your Motivational DNA
www.strengthsfinder.com - with purchase of book you get access to their strengths finder survey.

Notes

1. "Extreme Space" Space Science accessed on February 10, 2011, http://www.esa.int/esaSC/SEM75BS1VED_exreme_0.html.

2. David Stoop, *You Are What You Think* (Grand Rapids, MI: Fleming H. Revell, a Division of the Baker Publishing Group, 2009) 102.

3. Laura Whitworth, et.al. *Co-Active Coaching* (Mountain View, CA: Davies-Black Publishing, a Division of CPP, Inc., 2007).

4. Whitworth, *"Co-Active Coaching"*, 247.

5. Whitworth, *"Co-Active Coaching"*, 248.

6. Whitworth, *"Co-Active Coaching"*, 247.

7. Ryan Blair, *My Rules To Live By* (Audio CD, Visalus Sciences Success Club, December, 2009).

8. Marcus A. Buckingham and Donald O. Clifton, PhD. *Now Discover Your Strengths* (New York: Free Press, 2001), 72.

9. Buckingham, *"Now, Discover Your Strengths"*, 75.

10. Buckingham, *"Now, Discover Your Strengths"*, 69.

11. Buckingham, *"Now, Discover Your Strengths"*, 73.

12. Buckingham, *"Now, Discover Your Strengths"*, 71.

13. Focus on the Family. *Truth Project* (A production of Focus on the Family, 2006).

14. John Maxwell, *Talent Is Never Enough* (Nashville, TN: Thomas Nelson, Inc., 2007), 38.

15. Dale Brown, *Words To Lift Your Spirits* (Baton Rouge, LA: Dale Brown Enterprises, Inc.), 10.

16. Jim Rohn, *Excerpts from Jim Rohn Classic Collection* (Success Magazine Audio CD, February, 2010). Quotes by Jim Rohn, America's Foremost Business Philosopher, reprinted with permission from Jim Rohn International 2010. As a world- renowned author and success expert, Jim Rohn touched millions of lives during his 46 year career as a motivational speaker and messenger of positive life change. For more information on Jim and his popular personal achievement resources or to subscribe to the weekly Jim Rohn Newsletter, visit www.JimRohn.com.

17. John Maxwell, *Talent Is Never Enough* (Nashville, TN: Thomas Nelson, Inc., 2007).

18. David Stoop, *You Are What You Think* (Grand Rapids, MI: Fleming H. Revell, a Division of Baker Publishing Group, 2009, 14th printing), 30.

19. Viktor Frankl, *"Man's Search for Meaning"* accessed on February 10, 2011, http://www.webwinds.com/frankl/quotes.htm.

20. "Systems Thinking" accessed on February 10. 2011, http://www. systems-thinking.org/loi/loi.htm.

21. Tamara Lowe, *Get Motivated* (New York: Doubleday, 2009), 17.

22. Lowe, *"Get Motivated"*, 22.

23. Lowe, *"Get Motivated"*, 24.

24. Lowe, *"Get Motivated"*, 52.

25. Lowe, *Get Motivated"*, 12.

26. "SMART Goals" SMART Goal Setting, accessed on February 10, 2011, http://www.smart-goals.org.

27. John Maxwell, *Talent Is Never Enough* (Nashville, TN: Thomas Nelson, Inc., 2007) 259.